Dance of the Woodland Spirits

Under old oaks, they glide,
With laughter as their guide.
Tiny flames dance in air,
Whirling without a care.

They stomp on top of leaves,
Whispers echo through eaves.
Rolling in moss so tender,
With antics they render.

Glimmers of joy in bloom,
Chasing away the gloom.
Winks and pokes like a game,
Not a spirit the same.

In the soft, dappled light,
They twist with pure delight.
A jig beneath the stars,
Nature's fun little czars.

Enchanted Underbrush

In a thicket thick and wide,
Squirrels try to hide,
While rabbits play peek-a-boo,
In a joyful crew.

Dancing on mushroom caps,
They gather for giggly laps.
With a tickle from a breeze,
Every moment's a tease.

Twirls of floating pollen,
Sweet laughter keeps calling.
Each bush a secret stage,
For whimsy to engage.

Amidst the tangled ferns,
A playful spirit churns.
Nature's winks abound here,
Cheeky and clear.

A Flirt with Nature's Veil

In a gown of leafy lace,
Nature wears a playful face.
With each flutter, a dance,
The trees invite a chance.

Rustles behind the bark,
With whispers that leave a mark.
Fluttering leaves conspire,
To spark a gentle fire.

In the shade, coy glances,
As flowers take their chances.
A bow here, a nod there,
Nature's flirty affair.

With sunlight peeking through,
Bashful blooms bid adieu.
Each sway and cheeky smile,
Brings a giggle worthwhile.

Beneath the Curtain of Green

In the woods where shadows tease,
Ferns dance lightly in the breeze.
Whispers of secrets, a playful game,
Leaves giggle softly, calling your name.

A squirrel winks from a nearby branch,
As birds chirp tales of a daring romance.
Underneath canopies that twist and twirl,
Nature's jesters put on a whirl.

Woodland Romance Unveiled

Mossy carpets hide the fun,
A bunny hops, thinks it's a pun.
Butterflies flutter, casting their spells,
While clever raccoons plot giggling wells.

The trees lean in, sharing a jest,
Nature's laughter is truly the best.
With every rustle and wagging tail,
Woodland whispers spin quite the tale.

Flirting with the Forest

Dandelions toss their heads up high,
Swaying and waving as bees buzz by.
In every nook, there's a chuckle or grin,
The forest woos back, it's quite the win.

A toad croaks out a ribbit of charm,
As ladybugs convene, a parade alarm.
But even the leaves know how to tease,
Tickled by breezes, swaying with ease.

A Serenade in Green

Under the ferns, a picnic laid,
Ticklish leaves join the serenade.
Chirps and clicks, a woodland band,
Laughter erupts across the land.

The sun plays peek-a-boo, a sly rogue,
While shadows dance in a funny vogue.
In this green realm, joy takes flight,
As nature's quirks steal the spotlight.

Laughter in the Latticework of Life

In a garden of giggles where shadows play,
Little green dancers sneak in the fray.
They twirl in the breeze with a mischievous wink,
Whispering secrets that make the heart sink.

Symphonies of Swaying Fronds

Listen close to the rustle, a tickle of cheer,
Each leaf sings a tune that can brighten the year.
With a bounce and a sway, they play hide and seek,
Tickling toes as they dance, oh so cheeky and sleek.

Whimsy of the Woodland Charm

Among the tall timber, the tales come alive,
Where ivy and laughter unashamedly thrive.
Frogs in tuxedos croak jokes on a log,
While rabbits in hats give a nod and a smog.

Tender Twists of Nature

In nature's own theater, each twist has a flair,
With vines wrapping puns in a playful affair.
Oh, the glee of the green as it grows all around,
A comedy show, where the laughter is found.

Flirts of the Forest Floor

In a green dress, no less,
Fern sways with finesse.
Bugs whisper, oh so sly,
While leaves giggle nearby.

Dancing with whimsical grace,
Winks from the grassy space.
A squirrel chews and snickers,
Plant life sharing quick flickers.

The sun "accidentally" spills,
Golden laughs and merry thrills.
Bees buzz with a cheeky cheer,
Nature's flirtations appear.

With each rustle, they tease,
A game played by the breeze.
In this forest world so tight,
Every glance is pure delight.

A Serenade of Shadows

Beneath the trees, a playful scene,
Shadows twirl, bright and green.
Winking leaves, a gentle spark,
As moonlit nights play the lark.

In the silence, whispers hum,
As twigs crack, oh what fun!
A critter's nod, a sly retreat,
In this dance, all are discreet.

Twilight teases with its charm,
Nature's chorus, oh so warm.
Every rustle, every sway,
Hints of jokes they dare not say.

Laughter echoes, softly shared,
In their flirty winks, they dared.
The night conceals a playful wink,
In shadowed spaces, hearts will link.

Enchantment Along the Path

Frolicsome ferns line the trail,
With little secrets, they regale.
A squirrel chuckles, leaps with glee,
A hidden message, come and see!

Beneath the arch of leafy love,
A fluttering whisper floats above.
Cute critters chase with a grin,
In the tangle, antics begin.

Pigeons coo a fanciful tune,
While daisies delight in the moon.
Blades of grass sway with delight,
Crafting tales throughout the night.

Every step is a cheeky jest,
Nature's jesters, doing their best.
Join the revelry, don't be shy,
Where laughter lingers; oh my, oh my!

Flirtations in Ferny Glades

In a glade where secrets bloom,
Ferns flirt and scatter the gloom.
Whispers float on a gentle breeze,
As branches sway with playful tease.

A rabbit hops, a wink of a tail,
In their game, none will fail.
Pollen dances like gossiping friends,
Where nature's humor never ends.

With each rustle, giggles ignite,
In the quiet corners of the night.
The shadows embrace with a spin,
Swaying to the rhythm of whimsical din.

Join the jolly, the flora's gleam,
In this merry, green daydream.
Flirtations weave in laughter's grace,
In ferny glades, we find our place.

Whispers of the Shaded Grove

In the grove where shadows twine,
The leaves giggle, how divine!
A squirrel winks at passing bees,
While squirrels dance with graceful ease.

The sunlight plays hide and seek,
Feeling bold, the bunnies peek.
A hedgehog jives, his spines all prance,
In this wild and leafy dance.

Rabbits spill their tales of fun,
While chasing rays of golden sun.
The mushrooms nod with clownish flair,
In the laughter of the air.

Beneath the trees, a party starts,
Where twirling flora steals our hearts.
With chatter soft and whispers sweet,
Nature hosts this funny feat.

Secrets in the Underbrush

In hidden nooks where critters scamper,
Frogs perform their nightly pamper.
The badgers plot their silly schemes,
While fireflies dance in glowing dreams.

A snail on stilts walks oh-so-slow,
As crickets cheer, "Just go, go, go!"
The bushes sway with secret tales,
As laughter echoes through the trails.

Rabbits in suits play cards and dice,
While owls offer their sage advice.
The hedges gossip in hushed tones,
As raccoons strike their playful poses.

Every thicket holds a laugh,
With snickers shared on nature's path.
In this brush, so wild and lush,
The secrets spill in joyful hush.

Dances Amongst the Fronds

Underneath the leafy boughs,
The garden hosts a merry house.
Lizards twirl in greenish tights,
While ladybugs join in delights.

The ferns wear crowns of morning dew,
As butterflies swirl, quite the view.
Chirping tunes on tiny strings,
A band of bees begins to sing.

Earthworms slink in disco moves,
While beetles show their funky grooves.
A family of ants forms a line,
All marching in a dance divine.

With petals soft, they take the stage,
As blooms erupt no matter the age.
This forest floor, a dance so bold,
In verdant halls, their stories told.

Liaisons of the Lush Canopy

High above in green retreats,
Where sunlight melts and laughter beats.
Monkeys swing with silly grins,
Flipping through the leaves like twins.

Parrots squawk their gossip loud,
While toucans charm the feathered crowd.
Each branch a stage for crafty plots,
As nature brews its tangled knots.

Squirrels flirt with acorn dreams,
While sloths ponder life's simple themes.
With every rustle, a new game starts,
In this canopy of playful hearts.

Daffy dances as shadows sway,
In leafy halls they laugh and play.
A jester's smile upon each leaf,
In this green world, find sweet relief.

Rhythms of Rooted Dreams

In secret groves the ferns prance,
Tickled by the breezy chance.
They wiggle stems in playful cheer,
As if they've sipped on laughter's beer.

With every sway a giggle grows,
The breeze confides what no one knows.
Frogs roll their eyes, they take a stand,
While ferns revolt and start a band.

Each sprout a note, each leaf a beat,
They tap dance soft on little feet.
Nature's chorale, a vibrant tease,
The roots beneath sway with unease.

So if you stroll where green things play,
Catch their joke, let laughter sway.
For in the woodland's winking gleam,
Lie rhythms of our rooted dream.

Secrets Caught in the Briar

Amidst the thorns, the whispers spread,
Of ferns in fancy, secrets bred.
A dance of shadows, sharp and sly,
Where love notes flutter, oh, my, oh, my!

The bumblebees with gossip hum,
While creeping vines join in the fun.
They tickle hides and tease the light,
A riotous ball from day till night.

Lovers meet in tangled bows,
As bravery runs in leafy rows.
With each flirt trying to outshine,
It's a riot wrapped in nature's vine.

In hidden nooks, delight awaits,
With sighs and wings, it oscillates.
So tread with care, and hear them share,
The secrets caught in the bramble snare.

Fragrant Promises of the Wild

A wild bouquet, fresh scents arise,
With ferns on stage, they improvise.
They twirl and spin with carefree grace,
Promising joy in every space.

Each petal's wink, a jest so sly,
Inviting smiles as they pass by.
Nature's jesters with a green flair,
With fragrant dreams spread through the air.

Oh, how they tease with earthy breath,
Whispering tales of life and death.
Rollicking woos from roots so bright,
The sun spills laughter, a pure delight.

So frolic boldly through the glade,
Join ferns' chorus, do not fade.
In wild's embrace, where promises bloom,
Let giggles linger, dispel all gloom.

The Soft Gaze of Green Whispers

While soft green gazes peer around,
Whispers dance on the mossy ground.
A sloth on a branch gives a wink,
Ferns turn sly—oh, what do you think?

With sprightly hops, they shake their fronds,
In leafy jest, they start their bonds.
A mischievous breeze begins to tease,
Echoing life with giggles and ease.

Each plot entwined with playful blooms,
Sways in sync with the chortling rooms.
Dance like no one's watching, they dare,
Even the trees join in the affair.

So listen close, let laughter ring,
In nature's charm, feel what they bring.
For in the soft gaze of green whispers,
Lies a world where joy just simpers.

A Tangle of Tender Tendrils

In a garden bright and bold,
Where ferns and flirts both unfold,
Two leaves danced in playful glee,
Twirling 'round, as carefree as can be.

One leaf whispered to its friend,
'What mischief, shall we lend?
With sunlight bright, we'll sway and tease,
And charm the bugs upon the breeze.'

The Wild's Gentle Longing

Underneath the azure sky,
Ferns fancied birds that soared so high,
'Oh, to flap our fronds and fly!'
They giggled, plotting ways to try.

A squirrel passed, with a cheeky glance,
'Hey fronds, care to join my dance?
With nuts and leaves, we'll make a scene,
The quirkiest show the woods have seen!'

Whispers Among the Leaves

Amidst the ferns, secrets shared,
In hushed tones, none were spared,
'Look at that bug, he's such a clown,
Wearing a leaf for a silly crown!'

A bumblebee buzzed in disdain,
'You ferns are quite a funny chain!
With your pranks through sun and rain,
I am but a guest, your wild domain.'

Secrets of the Soft Green

Soft greens swayed, a giggly crew,
A playful breeze whispered too,
'Who's the fairest leaf of all?'
They cheered and shout, 'A fern's the call!'

With laughter bright, they held a show,
Where every leaf put on a glow,
With pokes and prods, they spun and twirled,
These soft green ferns, so fun unfurled!

Enchantment in Verdant Silhouettes

In the garden, ferns sway so bright,
Dressed in emerald, they dance in the light.
With a wink, they tease and they twirl,
Nature's jesters in a leafy swirl.

A breeze sends giggles through the fronds,
Whispering secrets in playful bonds.
Each leafy flirt, a wink in disguise,
Leaves us chuckling 'neath sunny skies.

They sway to the rhythm of nature's tune,
Courting the bees in the bright afternoon.
With rustles and tickles, they make us smile,
Transforming our stroll into a joyful mile.

As shadows stretch long, their laughter persists,
Witty and cheeky, they dance and insist.
In this verdant kingdom, love's silly game,
We'll giggle forever, never the same!

Fluttering Hearts of Green

Tiny ferns on a fluttering spree,
Winking at daisies, come dance with me!
Underneath boughs, they play hide and seek,
Growing bolder like youngsters, full of cheek.

Came a grasshopper, with a jump and a laugh,
Joined the ferns in a photo op path.
With a grin so wide, he smiled just right,
While ferns giggled softly at their green light.

Spirits lifted where mischief calls loud,
Ferns in formation, a quirky green crowd.
They whisper of tales with no care nor fuss,
While grinning from ear to ear—just us!

Twisting together like some leafy romance,
In shadows, they giggle, give love a chance.
With beats and flutters, they twist and they sway,
Creating a charm that will always stay!

Shadows and Sunbeams

Amidst the shadows, the ferns conspire,
With sunbeams above, they sparkle and aspire.
Playing tag with the light, oh what a sight,
Where greens flirt with gold in the warm daylight.

A squirrel pauses, its eyes open wide,
As the ferns toss jokes like leaves in a ride.
With a flick of their fronds, they shoo it away,
In a game of charades, come join in the play!

Underneath canopies, mischief resides,
The ferns share their laughter, where sunshine abides.
They roll in the grass, tickling the ground,
In a raucous affair where joy knows no bounds.

At twilight, the dance begins to unfold,
Ferns fluttering memories of young lips bold.
In this jungle of glee, where silliness beams,
They'll steal your heart with their whimsical schemes!

Courtship Beneath the Arching Leaves

Where the arching leaves form a delicate curtain,
The flirty ferns play, amid laughter uncertain.
A game of attraction in the soft evening glow,
They whisper sweet nothings, in breezy flow.

With each rustle and shiver, they strut and parade,
In this leafy bazaar, flirtation displayed.
Little critters gawk, big hearts on their sleeve,
As ferns craft a courtship you won't believe!

Under moonlight, they tap-dance on dew,
While critters eavesdrop on the leafy debut.
Giggles erupt as they twirl and caress,
In this garden of mischief, such joy to express.

As the night grows deep, their antics won't stop,
In these playful exchanges, no ferns are a flop.
Underneath archways of green, they'll play their hearts out,
In a courtship of laughter, that's what it's about!

Tangles in the Gentle Lush

In a garden where shadows play,
Two ferns met in a sprightly way.
They twirled around, oh what a sight,
Whispering secrets in soft moonlight.

One bragged about its leafy flair,
The other just laughed, "Do you really care?"
With fronds like fans, they flapped and swayed,
Creating a dance that time delayed.

They tangled up tight, in a leafy embrace,
Lost in laughter, oh what a race!
"You can't catch me!" one snickered with glee,
But both knew well, they'd roam wild and free.

As morning dew kissed their leaves with grace,
They posed for the sun, a leafy embrace.
In the greenwoods, love bloomed in the air,
With ferns flirting away without a care.

Expectation in the Forest's Heart

In the woods where the sunlight spills,
Two ferns planned mischief, oh what thrills!
They peered at a snail with curious intent,
"Will it race us?" one carefully sent.

Wagers were made as the stakes grew high,
With each tiny step, they let out a sigh.
The snail took its time, with calm aplomb,
While the ferns giggled, "This is so dumb!"

But patience they found was quite the charm,
As the ferns rooted down, oh so warm.
"Next time let's sprout legs, and we'll fly,
Instead of waiting for you to say bye!"

In the heart of the forest, dreams filled the air,
Each whisper shared, without a care.
Their hopes danced, a whimsical fling,
In the woods where ferns dreamt of spring.

Glimpses of Green Adoration

Amidst the glades, two ferns did spy,
A butterfly flaunting, oh so spry!
"Hey there, winged thing! Come take a seat,
We're the coolest greens you'll ever meet!"

The butterfly laughed, with colors so bright,
"You two leafy dancers make my day light!"
It twirled around, in a delicate race,
While ferns waved back with supreme grace.

Fronds brushed lightly in synchronized awe,
Charmed by colors and nature's law.
They planned a parade in the sunlight's glow,
Where every frond would steal the show.

A picnic was laid of dew and sunbeams,
With giggles and joys, beneath their dreams.
In the glades' whispers, they found their voice,
In the dance of green, they made their choice.

Secrets Beneath the Canopy

Beneath the vast and leafy crown,
Two ferns plotted in whispered tones.
"What if we start a rumor, how fun!"
"That squirrels wear hats, on the run!"

They giggled and snorted, shaking with glee,
Imagining squirrels with style and spree.
"And what of the rabbits? A royal scene,
Decked out in diamonds, oh so keen!"

Their laughter echoed through the leafy halls,
While nearby trees tried to stand tall.
"The world needs to know what we have found,
Secrets of style below the ground!"

As the forest listened, their spirits soared,
Ferns and their dreams, joyously adored.
In whispers of green, mischief was spun,
Creating a dance, oh how fun!

Romance of the Woodland Whisper

In the woods where giggles play,
Two trees dance in bright array.
They flirt with tips of leaves so bold,
Whispered secrets, stories told.

A squirrel winks from branch above,
While bees hum tunes of woodland love.
A dappled deer trots by with grace,
Nose crinkled in a playful chase.

The ground is soft with mossy dreams,
As sunbeams drop like whiskey streams.
Each twig a jester, full of cheer,
Nature's court jesters, oh so near.

They spin in circles, twirl and sway,
Mushrooms giggle in bright array.
With every rustle, laughter spryly,
The woodland whispers love so wily.

Verdant Vows and Soft Shadows

Under leaves, two shadows meet,
In a dance that's light and sweet.
Sweet grass tickles silly toes,
As laughter blooms like garden rose.

A branch bows low to hear the talk,
While daisies join in floral walk.
Promises made on the breeze,
Underneath the laughing trees.

The sun peeks in, a curious spy,
As butterflies flit, giggling by.
Frogs croak tunes of silly romance,
In this wild, playful woodland dance.

With every breeze, vows softly said,
Sprouts a chuckle, cradles a thread.
The soft shadows paint the hue,
Of woodland whimsies made for two.

The Language of Leaves

Leaves chatter in a joyous spree,
Translations lost to you and me.
A rustling pact, warmth in their tone,
Whispers found, and laughs well-known.

Saplings sway with youthful glee,
While elders nod vigorously.
They gossip sweet on summer's breath,
Plotting pranks, as time drips death.

From acorns dropped to dances wild,
Every green knuckle, nature's child.
Fingers of sunlight tickle nearby,
As frolicsome shadows giggle high.

Words take shape in the playful air,
In this woodland joy, a brilliance rare.
So, listen close, hear the leaves tease,
For nature's laughter puts hearts at ease.

Foliage Fantasies

In a world where greens conspire,
Each leaf a tale that will inspire.
A nutty jest from the mighty oak,
Where sunlight sprinkles laughter's cloak.

Tiny buds with jolly faces,
Greet the dawn in leafy places.
A dance of branches, sway and twirl,
Nature's laughter begins to whirl.

With a hint of mischief in their song,
The flora hums all day long.
A playful breeze joins in the fun,
As sunlight plays on everyone.

So gather round, let spirits lift,
In the woods, there's always a gift.
With flora dreams and whimsy neat,
Nature's humor can't be beat.

Infatuation in the Foliage

In shadows where the greens do play,
A shy leaf winked, 'Come out and sway!'
With whispered blush, the dew would cheer,
'This garden dance shall bring them near.'

Yet when the breeze began to tease,
The petals giggled, swayed with ease.
'Oh look, that stalk is really bold!'
'But wait, I've got another hold!'

To swoon by roots, in earth so rich,
With every wiggle, nature's pitch.
A tender glance, a rustling sigh,
We're tangled up—oh me, oh my!

Brushes of Nature's Affection

A frond painted green, oh what a sight,
It giggled with joy, a playful light.
"Oh darling sprout, come prance and play,
Your twisty charm makes my heart sway!"

With sheaths in place, they plotted and planned,
Creating mischief, so lively and grand.
"Hey there, grass, with your wild hair!
Join us in this leafy affair!"

A throw of shade, a patch of sun,
These entertaining plants just want fun.
Nature's bright comedy blooms each day,
In whispers and giggles, they prance away.

Sprigs of Sweet Anticipation

In the corner nook where sunlight spills,
Lies a fanciful sprig with fanciful thrills.
With playful jests, it beckons, "Hey,
Join in the fun—let's frolic and sway!"

Charmed by the whimsy of passing bees,
The petals danced softly, swaying with ease.
"Oh butterfly, come flutter and flirt,
Your colors bring life, oh, don't be hurt!"

With laughter that echoes through dampened air,
Every leaf twists in a humorous affair.
"Let's spin and twirl, oh let's not delay,
The nectar we share shall brighten the day!"

Whimsical Ways of the Underbrush

Down in the thicket, laughter resounds,
Where vines twist and tangle in playful bounds.
"Hey, little bud, don't you feel bold?
Let's make this underbrush story unfold!"

The thorns laughed with a prickly jest,
While blooms blossomed in fragrant fest.
"Oh thicket, oh wild, how we amuse!
With every rustle, we've got our muse!"

They played peek-a-boo beneath the ferns,
Chasing the wind with all of its turns.
A riot of giggles, this leafy array,
Whimsies galore in the bright light of day.

Liaisons in the Mossy Underworld

In the shadows where green things play,
The creatures dance in a cheeky ballet.
Mossy beds hide secrets untold,
While giggles of beetles begin to unfold.

A snail in a tux, ready to charm,
Whispers to grass without any harm.
Winks from the wilting wildflower bells,
Invite the shy mushrooms to share their spells.

Frogs in a chorus, croaking their tune,
Engage in a chat with the light of the moon.
Under the ferns, with a sly little grin,
Who knew the forest could be such a spin?

With vines like ribbons, and laughter like streams,
They spin silly stories of mossy daydreams.
In an underworld filled with playful delight,
Love notes on leaves make the evening just right.

The Art of Quiet Entanglement

In a patch where the wild things grow tall,
The shy ladybug takes a little fall.
With splashes of color, she blushes in style,
As the lanky grasshopper flashes a smile.

They whisper sweet nothings beneath leafy capes,
While fungi giggle in their mushroom-shaped drapes.
Oh, how they twirl in this tangled affair,
In a soft-green world without any care.

The lacy fronds wave in a whimsical way,
Encouraging chaos in nature's ballet.
As ants strut past with a flourish and sway,
Creating a ruckus while on their own way.

With roots intertwining, they share gentle sighs,
Plotting adventures 'neath the curious skies.
So gather your friends, let the laughter be loud,
In this court of green, let the quirks be proud!

Fables of the Forest Flocking

In the heart of the woods, birds gather and squawk,
Chasing after dreams in a round of a mock.
With feathers like paintbrushes on a grand site,
They brag about flights and their tales of delight.

A squirrel drops acorns in rhythmic refrain,
As patrons of foliage dance in the rain.
With whispers of breezes, the chatter takes flight,
In a theater of green where all acts feel right.

Bumblebees buzzing with humorous jives,
Swap stories of pollen and their funny lives.
A dapper young frog, in a waistcoat so fine,
Proposes a toast with a croak and a twine.

As sunbeams cascade through a canopy bright,
Each creature engages, reveling in light.
Fables are woven in this woodland delight,
With laughter and music making spirits take flight!

A Touch of Ferny Flirtation

In the cool, dappled shade where shadows expand,
Lively fronds flutter as if by their hand.
What secrets are hidden beneath all that green?
A bashful bouquet waits for a scene.

Charming old trees twist with giddy delight,
While playful vines sneak in close through the night.
A cricket crooning its longing refrain,
Spreading silly gossip with each gentle strain.

A waltz in the weeds pulls together a crowd,
As nature giggles, feeling lush and proud.
With laughter, they tumble in a whimsical rush,
Crafting their tales in a fidgety hush.

So here's to the moments wrapped up in the green,
To the flirtatious whispers in this lively scene.
Where everything dances with a cheeky flair,
The forest of fun invites hearts everywhere.

The Subtle Art of Seduction

In the garden, shadows play,
Leaves whisper secrets, come what may.
Crickets chuckle, butterflies tease,
Nature's antics put hearts at ease.

The daisies giggle, oh so bright,
Winking at bees with pure delight.
A ladybug struts, wearing its best,
While ants form a conga, never at rest.

The breeze brings laughter, a gentle tease,
As petals flutter with playful ease.
Catering to all who stroll by,
Love's a jest under the open sky.

In this realm where nature lies,
Flirtation blooms, oh how it flies!
From the tiniest sprout to the tallest tree,
Everyone's dancing, wild and free.

Nature's Flirtatious Dance

In meadows bright, the flowers sway,
Dancing close in a jocular display.
Bees bump and bounce, mischief in flight,
As petals twirl under sunlight.

The grass giggles, tickles the toes,
While ladybugs line up in rows.
A squirrel winks with a playful dart,
In this grand ballet, love's an art.

The clouds drift slow, a wink from above,
Nature's charms coax out all the love.
Branches entwine, a romantic twist,
A cuddle of roots, who could resist?

Life's a dance beneath the trees,
With laughter carried on the breeze.
So join the fun, don't miss your chance,
In nature's ball, come join the dance!

Swaying in Silent Harmony

In the hush of twilight, leaves converse,
Their whispers soft, like a light-hearted verse.
Breezes tease, playfully disrupt,
As mushrooms giggle in a damp little huddle.

Glimmers of sunlight sip on the dew,
Spouting tales of a love that's true.
A shadow passes, a flirt from the past,
In this green world, good times are vast.

The ferns lean close, giving side-eyed glances,
Inviting others to join their prances.
While twilight stirs, their laughter grows,
A symphony played in leafy throes.

In silent harmony, secrets bloom,
As giggles echo through nature's room.
So sway along in this playful night,
As nature whispers, everything feels right.

Secrets Shared in Shaded Nooks

In hidden corners where shadows peek,
Nature shares the sweetest cheek.
A squirrel blushes, hiding its stash,
As petals giggle, spilling the bash.

Underneath the branches, stories unfold,
Of daring love and secrets bold.
The dewdrops twinkle like stars anew,
As whispers of romance flow like morning dew.

A butterfly flirts, its colors so bright,
Entices the flowers; what a sight!
Grasshoppers chuckle, the frogs serenade,
In this garden party, love's parade!

So lean in close and hear the tales,
Of flirty ferns and loving snails.
In shaded nooks, laughter's the key,
As nature's charm plays, wild and free.

Hearts Entwined in Greenery

In a garden of secrets, they play,
Whispers of laughter dance on the sway,
With every twist, a grin does grow,
Beneath canopies, hearts in tow.

Leaves serve as a stage for their winks,
Mischief hidden, or so it thinks,
A bashful bow, a giggle shared,
In the shade where no one's dared.

Petals break rules of the formal ties,
Frolic and fun in disguise,
Nature's stage, like a grand ballet,
Two hearts leap, come what may.

In rustling green, love takes a chance,
Flirting with ferns in a lively dance,
With a hint of blush and cheeky tease,
They twirl together on a whimsical breeze.

The Hidden Glades of Longing

Among the shrubs, a secret lair,
Where lovebirds share a goofy stare,
In vibrant hues, they spin and leap,
While shyly hiding, hearts they keep.

Beneath the shade, soft chuckles burst,
Their playful glances, a joke rehearsed,
Whispers climb like wild vines stance,
A gleeful pause in a bashful dance.

Laughter echoes through shady lanes,
In this realm of tickles and gains,
Their stories tangled, just like the leaves,
Crafting tales that the fern world weaves.

With every rustle, their joy ignites,
Amongst the fronds of silly delights,
In hidden glades, with hearts in flight,
They chase the shadows, weaving bright.

Breezes Weaving Through Ferns

Gentle winds weave through lush green tails,
Whispers of jest between delicate veils,
Two souls grinning as they sway,
In playful dances, they find their way.

Giggling leaves tell tales of woe,
As hearts entwine in breezy flow,
Each gust brings warmth, the sun's embrace,
In the company of laughter, they find their place.

Chasing shadows, they sneak a peek,
With every rustle, their spirits peak,
Flirting with ferns, in teasing grace,
Nature's comedy, a whimsical chase.

With every twist, the laughter grows,
In this green realm, the heart's theater shows,
In breezes soft, their whispers play,
Two merry souls in fern-like ballet.

Echoes of a Shy Embrace

Amidst the greens, they often hide,
Ferns laugh along with hearts open wide,
A shy embrace in a leafy nook,
With each glance, their funny book.

Bumbling whispers swirl through the air,
As they trip over roots, unaware,
With giggles bursting like springtime blooms,
In their fortress of ferns, romance looms.

With playful jests and teasing glances,
They tread lightly on heart's advances,
In tangled vines, their secrets flow,
Love's comedy in the soft afterglow.

In quiet corners, chuckles rise,
With mossy hugs and sparkling eyes,
Echoes of joy in ferny disguise,
Two hearts entwined, underneath the skies.

Gossamer Threads of a Hidden Romance

In the garden, secrets play,
Whispers of love in a leafy sway.
Beneath the fronds, jesters hide,
Tickling the ferns, it's quite a ride.

Two leaves dance in the gentle breeze,
Sharing laughter beneath the trees.
A beetle's waltz, a cricket's song,
In this green world, they both belong.

Fluttering hearts among the green,
A couple tangled, sights unseen.
Ticklish tendrils, playful cheer,
What a time to be alive here!

Who knew romance could be so spry,
With dancing spores that flutter by?
In this whimsical, leafy space,
Love's a game, just pick your place!

Silhouettes in the Twilight

As the day bids a funny adieu,
Shadows stretch, a comical crew.
Laughter bounces off the dusk,
While ferns whisper, oh what a fuss!

A pair of sprites behind a leaf,
Keeping secrets, denying grief.
They poke their heads, all shy and bold,
Catching glimpses of tales untold.

Twilight giggles hide in the glade,
Frolicsome ferns and a masquerade.
With each rustle, a chuckle flows,
In this twilight, romance grows!

Just two silhouettes, laughter in tow,
Waltzing softly, stealing the show.
A blurry romance, sweet and bright,
In the laughter of a magical night!

The Lure of Lush Canopies

Underneath the vibrant leaves,
Nature teases, it never grieves.
A squirrel winks as he scampers high,
While lovers giggle and catch their sigh.

A hidden nook with colors so bright,
Frothy greenery, such a sight!
They tickle the tendrils, soft and green,
In this lush realm, they reign supreme.

Curly ferns and playful sights,
Whimsical glances in joyful flights.
Lovers flutter, mischief abounds,
In the dappled light, laughter resounds.

Every rustle promises a spark,
In the canopy where dreams embark.
Two hearts twirling in playful grace,
In the embrace of this verdant space!

Echoes of Soft Footfalls

Through the thicket, soft footfalls creep,
A pair of lovers, their secrets they keep.
With every step, ferns gently sway,
Echoes of laughter lead the way.

In a chorus of chirps, they whisper and jest,
Among the foliage, they feel blessed.
A snippet of humor in breezy flight,
Dancing like shadows in fading light.

With every rustling leaf, there's a tease,
Playing footsie with the nimble breeze.
In the heart of the wild, they twine and twirl,
Where ferns flirt and laughter unfurl.

Oh, those echoes in the peaceful night,
Humor mingling in pure delight.
In the company of greens, they find,
A fabled love, uniquely entwined!

Moorland Murmurs of Affection

Whispers dance on breezy hills,
A cheeky breeze gives silly chills.
Frolicsome ferns in playful spread,
Tickle the toes of those who tread.

Banter blooms where the cuckoo calls,
Among the rocks, friendship sprawls.
Jests are passed from leaf to leaf,
In this green patch of comic relief.

Sunlight sprinkles on emerald beds,
With laughter sprouting from our heads.
We trip on roots, but spirits rise,
In this land of bright, teasing skies.

Each rustle hints of secrets shared,
In a world that's whimsically bared.
So let us leap and let us laugh,
In moorland's sweet, flirtatious half.

Thickets of Timid Touches

Behind the leaves, a blush appears,
A stolen glance, an echo of cheers.
Beneath the boughs, we play a game,
Where fumbling fingers spark the flame.

In shadows deep where giggles hide,
We share our thoughts with giddy pride.
A rustling kiss, then swift retreat,
As shy hearts race in rhythmic beat.

Branches arch like sheltering arms,
Inviting us to share our charms.
Oh, the flutters of tender lore,
In this thicket, we long for more.

With every turn, our spirits leap,
A secret world where we can keep.
Timid touches, a merry chase,
In the thicket, we find our place.

Serenading the Shaded Path

Under a bough, we hum and sway,
Singing soft tunes as children play.
Little whispers blend with song,
In a shaded path where we belong.

Sun-dappled laughter fills the air,
With every step, we dance with flair.
A playful poke, a gentle shove,
In this moment, we feel the love.

Where petals fall like stars from trees,
We jest and tease with joyful ease.
Each stride reveals a cheerful trick,
In our merriment, time feels thick.

So join the tune, let spirits lift,
With smiles exchanged, our sweetest gift.
A serenade beneath the sky,
As we whisper dreams and watch them fly.

Swaying in the Dappled Light

Dancing shadows, a playful sight,
We twirl and laugh in the dappled light.
Leaves overhead, they join our cheer,
As whispers flutter, drawing near.

Twirling ferns with a cheeky sway,
Invite us to join their hilarious play.
With every laugh, the world seems bright,
Swaying along in sheer delight.

In sunlit patches, our worries flee,
Where giggles entwine like roots of a tree.
Come, chase the giggles, don't be shy,
In this vibrant world, together we fly.

With every rustle that tickles the air,
We share our jokes with comic flair.
Swaying, we mingle, frolic, and float,
Amidst dappled light, love's funny note.

Heartbeats in the Hidden Grove

In a grove where shadows play,
Hearts race in a cheeky way.
Leaves rustle with a giggling sound,
As secrets dance upon the ground.

A dandelion twirls in delight,
Whispering dreams in the soft moonlight.
Bouncing ferns tease with a wave,
Silly romances, we crave to save.

Caught in a tangle of vines so sweet,
We laugh and stumble on our feet.
With every step, a heart skips fast,
Wondering, will this moment last?

But nature laughs, the breeze takes flight,
Leading us home into the night.
Yet, with each pulse in this grove,
Laughter blooms, as we dare to rove.

Timid Affections in Green Hues

Underneath the leafy canopy,
Shy whispers flutter, oh so fancy.
Blushes peek from emerald beds,
Soft smiles hidden, bashful heads.

A ladybug roams, seeking a friend,
While butterflies kindly pretend.
Wiggly worms with a twinkle in stare,
Might they just care? Do they dare?

Hiding behind a sturdy frond,
Two hearts beat, a timid bond.
Giggling sprites observe the scene,
In a textured world, sweet and green.

Beneath the ferns, a chuckle upsprings,
We're tangled in life's little flings.
With timid thrills in this leafy spree,
We twirl and laugh, just wild and free.

Fleeting Glances Through Ferns

In a patch where ferns grow wild,
A peep here and there, oh how we smiled.
Eyes darting like mischievous sprites,
Fleeting moments, nature's delights.

One glance and then a swift retreat,
Nature's secret, the rhythm of beat.
Tickled hearts hide behind green veils,
Our giggles echo, as time prevails.

The sun winks through the leaf-lit scene,
Crafting a game, a playful routine.
Rustling leaves join in the tease,
A whirlwind of whispers in the breeze.

Just beyond the ferns' embrace,
Flirty laughter dances, keeps pace.
In this tangle, we just might find,
That playful love is one of a kind.

Nebulous Hues of Nature's Charm

In a world where colors mingle,
Nature's laughter makes our hearts tingle.
Dappled greens and sunlit browns,
A canvas of joy, no time for frowns.

Wobbly daisies bob with glee,
Ferns giggle as they sway for me.
With every step, the ground's alive,
A symphony where we thrive.

Each shade a note, a tune so sweet,
As we chirp, skip, and dance our feet.
With every breath, we taste the bliss,
In this living world, a playful kiss.

So let the colors paint our fate,
With silly stumbles that feel so great.
Wrapped in blooms of nature's spell,
We're caught in charm, oh can you tell?

A Song of the Soft Earth

In the garden, green things sway,
Whispering secrets all day.
The soil giggles with delight,
As worms dance under moonlight.

Dancing leaves tickle the breeze,
Swaying gently with such ease.
Bugs wearing tiny top hats,
You can't help but laugh at that!

Raindrops fall like playful chimes,
Setting the stage for good times.
Nature's got a sense of play,
Let's join in, hip-hip-hooray!

So here's to the ground so soft,
Where joys are never far off.
Join the fun, it's such a treat,
In this earth dance, our hearts meet.

Echoes of the Forest Floor

Crunching twigs underfoot, so fun,
As squirrels plot, oh what a run!
Leaves chatter in playful jest,
While mushrooms wear their finest vest.

The owls hoot like old-time crooners,
As woodpeckers join in, real tuners.
Badgers in their sneaky games,
Stealthy shuffles, wild wild names!

Sunbeams peek through branches high,
Spotting antics in the sky.
The forest floor is full of cheer,
Nature's laugh is loud and clear!

So come and wander, take it slow,
Join the creatures, steal the show!
In this realm of woodland lore,
We'll giggle and play forevermore.

A Serenade of Swaying Foliage

Wavy greens with a charming pose,
Swishing lightly, tickling toes.
Each leaf laughs as breezes blow,
In leafy skirts, they put on a show!

Dancing non-stop in the sun,
Who knew that plants could be this fun?
With nature's rhythm, they won't stop,
Swinging around, ready to hop!

Giggling flowers, bright and loud,
Drawing in each curious crowd.
Chasing shadows, twisting bright,
With every turn, what a sight!

So hear the calls from branches high,
In foliage, our spirits fly.
Nature's chorus sings with glee,
In this world, let's dance so free!

Nature's Subtle Allure

Breezes tease with playful sighs,
Nature's charm hides in her guise.
A wink from petals, soft and sweet,
With a giggle, they skip and greet!

The sun peeks through with a cheeky grin,
Unveiling the joy that's deep within.
The squirrels prance and walls encroach,
As fungi wear a wise old broach!

Rippled streams that splash and laugh,
Twist and turn, a playful path.
Joyous whispers through the pines,
Each rustle shares the silliest lines!

So here we dance among the greens,
In nature's realm, where laughter beams.
With funny little friends we find,
Life's most precious, gentle kind!

Nature's Gentle Pursuit

In the garden, plants sway and play,
Tiny critters dance, then stray.
A butterfly winks, takes flight,
While ants argue who's the might.

A leaf whispers secrets, oh so sly,
As dandelions giggle and sigh.
The bees buzz in a merry tune,
While frogs croak under the silver moon.

Petals blush, blush like a teen,
While a grasshopper leaps, feeling keen.
Nature's courtship in bright array,
Flirting in a whimsical ballet.

Clouds drift by, in the sky they flit,
As dew drops nod, they won't omit.
Every moment sparking delight,
Nature's humor, a buzzing kite.

Lush Layers of Unsung Love

Beneath the ferns, secrets unfold,
Where tales of romancing are often told.
Mushrooms giggle in the damp ground,
While evening shadows swirl around.

A squirrel with charm, with a cheeky grin,
Nibbles on acorns, like it's a sin.
The daisies whisper, 'Can we dance?'
While the wind giggles at their prance.

Wiggling worms enjoy a chat,
In a soil café beneath the mat.
With rosy cheeks, the violets tease,
As ants parade, strutting with ease.

In this lush realm, miracles are few,
Yet laughter bursts forth, as if on cue.
Nature's jesters in colors bright,
All sharing in the fun, what a sight!

Labyrinths of Leafy Longing

In a maze of leaves, a ticklish breeze,
Rustles the branches, makes the trees sneeze.
A chubby hedgehog rolls with flair,
Tumbling down without a care.

A fox in boots struts with pride,
Tail high, in nature's joyful ride.
Berries blush, wearing a crown,
While twigs crack jokes, they won't frown.

Ferns wave hello, all fresh and green,
While a snail slips past, not too keen.
In this labyrinth, flavors collide,
As laughter echoes from every side.

A squirrel-swinging dance routine,
Leaves the audience feeling keen.
In this leafy haven, fun's anew,
Where six-legged romancers continue to woo.

Echoes of Enchantment

In the twilight, shadows prance,
Nature's critters get lost in a dance.
Fireflies twinkle, winking bright,
While crickets chirp into the night.

An owl shrieks, 'What's all the fuss?'
While the parched earth says, 'Hey, discuss!'
The roses laugh in sweet harmony,
As the thorns poke back mischievously.

With a splash, the pond reflects the sky,
As frogs croak loud, giving it a try.
An acorn spins, feeling quite grand,
As the sun sinks low, on the land.

Every insect hums a catchy tune,
Crafting night's laughter beneath the moon.
In this magic of nature's own song,
Echoes of enchantment all night long.

The Pulse of the Wild Heart

In the glade where shadows wink,
Dancing leaves and laughter blink,
A little critter steals the show,
With every twist, it steals the dough.

A squirrel struts with style so grand,
It prances 'round, a furry band,
The branches shake, the birds take flight,
All join the fun in sheer delight.

With acorns tossed like hot confetti,
It's a party, never petty,
They twirl and leap, a merry bunch,
Their antics make us laugh and crunch.

In wild heartbeats, joy's the song,
Where laughter lives the whole day long,
Among the trees, we find our part,
A chorus loud, the wild heart's art.

A Canvas of Nature's Attire

In leafy gowns of green so bright,
The forest dresses day and night,
With blossoms dancing on the breeze,
Nature struts with stylish ease.

A flower blushes, coy and shy,
Practicing looks as bees fly by,
A tulip sighs, 'Oh, take me home!'
While daisies plot in fragrant foam.

Vines whisper tales in swirls and curls,
Chatting softly with the pearls,
Of dew that clings on morning's face,
Each drop a giggle in this place.

And here we stand, all bright and spry,
With nature's art, we dance and fly,
In this attire, both bold and sweet,
Life paints us with a playful beat.

Flirtation in the Fragrant Thicket

In thickets thick where secrets play,
A sleepy bee steals hearts away,
With tiny wings and charming spins,
It flirts with blooms, where fun begins.

A fern says, 'Oh, look at me!'
With fronds that flutter, wild and free,
While roses giggle, red-faced bright,
In the thicket's daring light.

The daisies wink, the violets tease,
All join the dance in gentle breeze,
A rustle here, a chuckle there,
Nature's flirts have not a care.

In fragrant air, the laughter swells,
Where every petal knows and tells,
Of flirtatious sways and dances,
Encapsulating sweet romances.

Heartstrings of the Herbal Haven

In the garden's heart, a silly tune,
Herbs are giggling under the moon,
Mint whispers secrets, thyme rolls its eyes,
While basil dons its best disguise.

Rosemary struts with a sway so fine,
Sage throws a party, 'come dine, come dine!'
With laughter steeped in playful cheer,
Their herbal humor fills the air clear.

Oregano elbows poor dill on edge,
They laugh together, and then they pledge,
To spice it up, the night is young,
With every joke, the joy is sung.

In this haven of nature's delight,
Heartstrings tangle, laughter takes flight,
With herbal whispers and cheeky grins,
In this merry dance, the fun begins.

Fluttering Hearts Beneath the Fronds

In a garden where giggles play,
Little ferns sway and dance all day.
With leafy whispers and cheeky grins,
They poke at lovers beneath their skins.

One cheeky shoot gave a playful nudge,
Sending a couple to stumble and fudge.
They laughed out loud at the fern's bold tease,
While ferns chuckled softly in the breeze.

Breezes That Caress

Winds whisk the leaves like a secret song,
Making hearts flutter, it won't be long.
A rustle, a tickle, then giggles emerge,
As ferns wink conspiracies, love at their verge.

A flutter here, a nudge from there,
The lovers look around, wonder with flair.
"Oh, was that you?" they giggle in mirth,
As the breezes brings joy, a light-hearted birth.

Winks in the Woodland

Through a thicket where sprites often play,
Ferns roll their eyes in a flirty ballet.
They glance at the couples with mischief and jest,
Poking fun, stirring hearts, they know how to jest.

"Hey there, watch out!" one fern gave a shout,
As a lover spilled coffee, with laughter, no doubt.
"Nature's the matchmaker, we're simply the leaves,"
They wink at the couples, it's love that they weave.

Serendipity in Swaying Greens

In a grove where romance blooms bright,
Ferns sway lightly, teasing with delight.
With each gentle wave, a whisper of chance,
They stoke the sweet spark of an accidental romance.

"Oops, I tripped over roots!" someone cried,
As ferns shook their heads, like a playful guide.
"Blame it on us! We can't help but charm,
But look here, you're safe from any alarm."

A Rendezvous in the Understory

Two leaves danced with playful glee,
One whispered, "Come, twirl with me!"
A bug intrudes, with wiggly flair,
"Not now, dear friend, we're quite the pair!"

They rolled and tumbled, laughter flew,
A critter's giggle, what a crew!
With sunlight spilling through the trees,
Their frolics stirred the buzzing bees.

A squirrel peeked from up above,
Teasing the leaves with playful shove.
"You're quite the couple, don't you see?"
"Oh hush! We're just leaf-siblings, whee!"

As shadows stretched, they held on tight,
The forest sighed, it felt just right.
In a world of green, they spin and sway,
Life's a joke; let's laugh today!

Feathered Embrace of the Wild

Two birds flirted atop a moss,
One chirped loud, the other boss.
"Your feathers shine!", the first one sang,
"It's oil, my dear. Just watch it hang!"

With swoops and dives, they played tag,
They fluffed and strutted, giving a brag.
A sly rabbit watched from the grass,
"Oh look, it's love, or just some sass!"

They chirped and bickered, a comic show,
First one would flaunt, then the other would go.
With every twist and every turn,
The forest laughed; oh, how they yearn!

At dusk they perched, with hearts aglow,
Giggling softly, adieu to the show.
Underneath stars, they made a pact,
To keep the fun—forever intact!

Green Whispers of Intrigue

In the shady realm where secrets sway,
A mouse proposed a game one day.
He'd challenge the frog to leap and croak,
"A most hilarious, cheeky poke!"

They gathered friends, the scene was set,
A betting game, no chance for regret.
The turtle watched, with a knowing grin,
"This will be rich! Let the games begin!"

With a leap and a ribbit, the contest ignites,
With giggles and snickers, illuminating nights.
The grasshoppers jumped, cheering on the show,
"Who will win? The frog or the foe?"

As laughter echoed through the glen,
The match went on—again and again!
With each little slip and flurry of feet,
All trivial matters turned to pure sweet.

Moonlit Meetings Amidst the Greens

By the moon's glow, the crickets convene,
An owl asked, "What's this late-night scene?"
A toad replied, with a wink of delight,
"Just a gathering; join our light!"

They danced in circles, all in a row,
A whirlwind of joy, in the glimmering glow.
The bushes rustled, a fox sighed with cheer,
"What a ruckus! I must join here!"

With songs and whispers, the night passed fast,
Stories and giggles—a brave spell cast.
The stars blinked down, watching the cheer,
"A midnight ball, how clever, my dear!"

As dawn approached, the laughter did fade,
Yet memories lingered of the fun they'd made.
In the heart of the woods, a promise stayed,
To meet again, where the coolness played!

www.ingramcontent.com/pod-product-compliance
Lightning Source LLC
Chambersburg PA
CBHW051633160426
43209CB00004B/626